50 Holiday Treats to Share

By: Kelly Johnson

Table of Contents

- Peppermint Bark
- Gingerbread Cookies
- Eggnog Cheesecake Bars
- Sugar Cookie Snowflakes
- Chocolate-Dipped Pretzels
- Cranberry Orange Bread
- Spiced Pecan Clusters
- Mini Pumpkin Pies
- Snickerdoodle Bars
- Fudge with Marshmallow Swirls
- Chocolate Crinkle Cookies
- Cinnamon Roll Bites
- White Chocolate Cranberry Blondies
- Peppermint Chocolate Truffles
- Apple Cider Donuts
- Holiday Fruitcake
- Hot Cocoa Mix Jars
- Chocolate Toffee Bark
- Cherry Almond Biscotti
- Pecan Pie Bars
- Eggnog Truffles
- Molasses Cookies
- Salted Caramel Brownies
- Candy Cane Macarons
- Hazelnut Chocolate Tartlets
- Gingerbread Fudge
- Caramel Pecan Pretzel Bites
- Mini Cheesecakes with Cranberry Sauce
- Poppy Seed Lemon Muffins
- Spiced Hot Chocolate Cookies
- Chai Spiced Cupcakes
- Cinnamon Sugar Roasted Nuts
- Maple Glazed Donuts
- Almond Joy Fudge
- Roasted Chestnuts

- Holiday Cake Pops
- Cranberry Pistachio Shortbread
- Chocolate Peppermint Whoopie Pies
- Pumpkin Spice Truffles
- Butterscotch Pretzel Cookies
- Sweet Potato Pie Bars
- Mocha Mint Brownies
- Eggnog Panna Cotta
- Cranberry Meringue Cookies
- Chocolate-Covered Caramel Apples
- Spiced Apple Cider Caramels
- Mint Chocolate Chip Cookies
- Cranberry Coconut Macaroons
- Chocolate Dipped Fruit
- Festive Marzipan Treats

Peppermint Bark

Ingredients:

- 12 oz dark chocolate, chopped
- 12 oz white chocolate, chopped
- 1/2 tsp peppermint extract
- 1/2 cup crushed peppermint candies

Instructions:

1. **Melt the dark chocolate**: In a heatproof bowl, melt the dark chocolate over a double boiler or in the microwave in 30-second intervals, stirring after each. Once melted, stir in the peppermint extract.
2. **Spread the dark chocolate**: Pour the melted dark chocolate onto a parchment-lined baking sheet and spread it into an even layer. Let it set in the refrigerator for about 20 minutes.
3. **Melt the white chocolate**: Melt the white chocolate the same way, then pour it over the set dark chocolate layer. Swirl the two chocolates together with a knife for a marbled effect.
4. **Top with peppermint**: Sprinkle the crushed peppermint candies over the top.
5. **Set and break**: Refrigerate until fully set (about 1 hour). Break into pieces and serve.

Gingerbread Cookies

Ingredients:

- 3 cups all-purpose flour
- 1 tsp baking soda
- 1 tbsp ground ginger
- 1 tsp cinnamon
- 1/2 tsp cloves
- 1/2 tsp salt
- 3/4 cup unsalted butter, softened
- 1/2 cup brown sugar
- 1 egg
- 1/2 cup molasses
- 1 tsp vanilla extract

Instructions:

1. **Preheat the oven**: Set the oven to 350°F (175°C). Line baking sheets with parchment paper.
2. **Mix dry ingredients**: In a bowl, whisk together the flour, baking soda, ginger, cinnamon, cloves, and salt.
3. **Cream butter and sugar**: In another bowl, cream together the butter and brown sugar until fluffy. Beat in the egg, molasses, and vanilla extract.
4. **Combine**: Gradually add the dry ingredients to the wet ingredients, mixing until smooth.
5. **Chill the dough**: Roll the dough into a ball, wrap in plastic wrap, and chill for at least 1 hour.
6. **Shape and bake**: Roll out the dough on a floured surface to 1/4 inch thick. Cut out shapes and place on baking sheets. Bake for 8-10 minutes or until firm. Cool completely before decorating.

Eggnog Cheesecake Bars

Ingredients:

- 1 ½ cups graham cracker crumbs
- 1/4 cup granulated sugar
- 1/2 cup unsalted butter, melted
- 16 oz cream cheese, softened
- 1 cup sour cream
- 3/4 cup granulated sugar
- 2 large eggs
- 1 tsp vanilla extract
- 1 tsp ground nutmeg
- 1/2 cup eggnog

Instructions:

1. **Make the crust**: Preheat the oven to 325°F (160°C). Mix graham cracker crumbs, sugar, and melted butter in a bowl. Press into the bottom of a greased 9x9-inch baking pan. Bake for 8-10 minutes, then let cool.
2. **Prepare the filling**: Beat cream cheese, sour cream, and sugar until smooth. Add the eggs one at a time, mixing well after each. Stir in the vanilla extract, nutmeg, and eggnog.
3. **Bake**: Pour the filling over the cooled crust. Bake for 35-40 minutes until set and slightly golden on top. Let it cool before refrigerating for at least 3 hours before serving.

Sugar Cookie Snowflakes

Ingredients:

- 2 ¾ cups all-purpose flour
- 1 tsp baking powder
- 1/2 tsp salt
- 1 cup unsalted butter, softened
- 1 ½ cups granulated sugar
- 1 large egg
- 1 tsp vanilla extract
- Icing for decoration (optional)

Instructions:

1. **Mix dry ingredients**: Whisk together the flour, baking powder, and salt in a bowl.
2. **Cream butter and sugar**: In a separate bowl, cream the butter and sugar until light and fluffy. Add the egg and vanilla extract, mixing until smooth.
3. **Combine**: Gradually add the dry ingredients to the wet mixture until a dough forms. Chill for at least 30 minutes.
4. **Roll out and cut**: Preheat the oven to 350°F (175°C). Roll out the dough on a floured surface to 1/4 inch thickness. Cut into snowflake shapes and place on a baking sheet.
5. **Bake**: Bake for 8-10 minutes or until the edges are lightly golden. Let cool before decorating with icing if desired.

Chocolate-Dipped Pretzels

Ingredients:

- 2 cups mini pretzels
- 1 cup dark or milk chocolate, melted
- Sprinkles or crushed candy canes for topping

Instructions:

1. **Melt the chocolate**: Melt the chocolate in a microwave or double boiler, stirring until smooth.
2. **Dip pretzels**: Dip each pretzel halfway into the melted chocolate, allowing any excess to drip off.
3. **Add toppings**: Place the dipped pretzels on parchment paper and sprinkle with festive toppings.
4. **Set**: Let the chocolate set in the refrigerator for about 30 minutes.

Cranberry Orange Bread

Ingredients:

- 2 cups all-purpose flour
- 1 ½ tsp baking powder
- 1/2 tsp baking soda
- 1/2 tsp salt
- 1 cup granulated sugar
- 1 large egg
- 1 cup fresh orange juice
- 1/4 cup unsalted butter, melted
- 1 tsp vanilla extract
- 1 cup fresh cranberries, chopped

Instructions:

1. **Preheat the oven**: Set the oven to 350°F (175°C). Grease a loaf pan.
2. **Combine dry ingredients**: In a bowl, whisk together the flour, baking powder, baking soda, salt, and sugar.
3. **Mix wet ingredients**: In another bowl, whisk together the egg, orange juice, butter, and vanilla extract.
4. **Combine and bake**: Gradually add the wet ingredients to the dry ingredients, mixing until just combined. Fold in the cranberries. Pour the batter into the prepared loaf pan and bake for 55-60 minutes. Let cool before serving.

Spiced Pecan Clusters

Ingredients:

- 1 cup pecan halves
- 1/2 cup granulated sugar
- 1 tsp ground cinnamon
- 1/2 tsp ground nutmeg
- 1/4 tsp ground cloves
- 1/4 tsp salt
- 1 tbsp unsalted butter

Instructions:

1. **Toast the pecans**: Preheat the oven to 350°F (175°C). Spread the pecans on a baking sheet and toast for 10-12 minutes.
2. **Coat with spices**: In a bowl, toss the pecans with sugar, cinnamon, nutmeg, cloves, and salt.
3. **Caramelize**: In a pan, melt the butter over medium heat. Add the spiced pecans and cook, stirring occasionally, for 5-7 minutes until caramelized. Let cool on parchment paper.

Mini Pumpkin Pies

Ingredients:

- 1 can (15 oz) pumpkin puree
- 1/2 cup heavy cream
- 1/2 cup brown sugar
- 2 large eggs
- 1 tsp ground cinnamon
- 1/2 tsp ground ginger
- 1/4 tsp ground nutmeg
- 1/4 tsp salt
- 1 package pie dough (store-bought or homemade)

Instructions:

1. **Preheat the oven**: Set the oven to 350°F (175°C). Grease a muffin tin.
2. **Make the filling**: In a bowl, mix the pumpkin puree, heavy cream, brown sugar, eggs, spices, and salt until smooth.
3. **Assemble the pies**: Roll out the pie dough and cut into rounds that fit the muffin tin. Press into the cups and fill with the pumpkin mixture.
4. **Bake**: Bake for 25-30 minutes or until set. Let cool before serving.

Snickerdoodle Bars

Ingredients:

- 2 ½ cups all-purpose flour
- 2 tsp cream of tartar
- 1 tsp baking soda
- 1/4 tsp salt
- 1 cup unsalted butter, softened
- 1 ½ cups granulated sugar
- 2 large eggs
- 1 tsp vanilla extract
- 3 tbsp sugar
- 2 tsp ground cinnamon

Instructions:

1. **Preheat the oven**: Set the oven to 350°F (175°C). Grease a 9x13-inch baking pan.
2. **Mix dry ingredients**: In a bowl, whisk together the flour, cream of tartar, baking soda, and salt.
3. **Cream butter and sugar**: In another bowl, beat together the butter and sugar until fluffy. Add the eggs and vanilla extract, mixing well.
4. **Combine and bake**: Gradually add the dry ingredients to the wet mixture. Spread the dough into the prepared pan. Mix the cinnamon and sugar and sprinkle over the top.
5. **Bake**: Bake for 25-30 minutes until golden brown. Let cool before cutting into bars.

Fudge with Marshmallow Swirls

Ingredients:

- 3 cups semi-sweet chocolate chips
- 1 can (14 oz) sweetened condensed milk
- 1/4 cup unsalted butter
- 1/2 tsp vanilla extract
- 1 1/2 cups mini marshmallows

Instructions:

1. **Melt the fudge**: In a medium saucepan, melt the chocolate chips, sweetened condensed milk, and butter over low heat, stirring constantly until smooth.
2. **Add vanilla**: Stir in the vanilla extract.
3. **Swirl in marshmallows**: Remove from heat and fold in the mini marshmallows, allowing them to swirl through the fudge mixture.
4. **Set the fudge**: Pour the fudge into a greased 9x9-inch pan and spread evenly. Refrigerate for 2 hours or until firm. Cut into squares and serve.

Chocolate Crinkle Cookies

Ingredients:

- 1 cup all-purpose flour
- 1/2 cup unsweetened cocoa powder
- 1 tsp baking powder
- 1/2 tsp salt
- 1/4 cup vegetable oil
- 1 cup granulated sugar
- 2 large eggs
- 1 tsp vanilla extract
- 1/2 cup powdered sugar (for rolling)

Instructions:

1. **Preheat the oven**: Set the oven to 350°F (175°C). Line baking sheets with parchment paper.
2. **Combine dry ingredients**: In a bowl, whisk together the flour, cocoa powder, baking powder, and salt.
3. **Mix wet ingredients**: In another bowl, beat the oil, granulated sugar, eggs, and vanilla until smooth.
4. **Combine**: Gradually add the dry ingredients to the wet ingredients, mixing until well combined. The dough will be thick.
5. **Shape the cookies**: Roll the dough into 1-inch balls, then roll each ball in powdered sugar to coat.
6. **Bake**: Place the balls on the prepared baking sheets, spacing them 2 inches apart. Bake for 10-12 minutes, or until the cookies have cracked on top. Let cool before serving.

Cinnamon Roll Bites

Ingredients:

- 1 can refrigerated cinnamon rolls (8-count)
- 1/4 cup unsalted butter, melted
- 1/2 tsp ground cinnamon
- 1/4 cup granulated sugar
- 1/4 cup cream cheese frosting (from the cinnamon roll package or homemade)

Instructions:

1. **Preheat the oven**: Set the oven to 375°F (190°C). Grease a muffin tin.
2. **Prepare the rolls**: Open the cinnamon roll package and cut each roll into 4 small pieces.
3. **Coat the dough**: In a bowl, mix the melted butter, cinnamon, and sugar. Toss the dough pieces in the cinnamon-sugar mixture until well coated.
4. **Bake**: Place the coated dough pieces in the muffin tin, filling each cup with about 4 pieces. Bake for 12-15 minutes, or until golden brown.
5. **Top with frosting**: Drizzle the cream cheese frosting over the warm cinnamon roll bites before serving.

White Chocolate Cranberry Blondies

Ingredients:

- 1 1/2 cups all-purpose flour
- 1 tsp baking powder
- 1/4 tsp salt
- 1/2 cup unsalted butter, melted
- 1 cup packed brown sugar
- 2 large eggs
- 1 tsp vanilla extract
- 1/2 cup dried cranberries
- 1 cup white chocolate chips

Instructions:

1. **Preheat the oven**: Set the oven to 350°F (175°C). Grease a 9x9-inch baking pan.
2. **Mix dry ingredients**: In a bowl, whisk together the flour, baking powder, and salt.
3. **Combine wet ingredients**: In another bowl, whisk together the melted butter and brown sugar. Add the eggs and vanilla extract, and beat until smooth.
4. **Add dry ingredients**: Gradually add the dry ingredients to the wet mixture, stirring until just combined.
5. **Add cranberries and white chocolate**: Fold in the dried cranberries and white chocolate chips.
6. **Bake**: Pour the batter into the prepared pan and bake for 25-30 minutes, or until a toothpick inserted in the center comes out clean. Let cool before slicing.

Peppermint Chocolate Truffles

Ingredients:

- 8 oz semi-sweet chocolate, chopped
- 1/2 cup heavy cream
- 1/2 tsp peppermint extract
- 1/4 cup crushed peppermint candies (for coating)

Instructions:

1. **Heat the cream**: In a saucepan, heat the heavy cream over medium heat until it begins to simmer. Remove from heat.
2. **Melt the chocolate**: Add the chopped chocolate to the warm cream and stir until smooth and fully melted.
3. **Flavor the truffles**: Stir in the peppermint extract. Let the mixture cool to room temperature, then refrigerate for about 1 hour or until firm.
4. **Form truffles**: Scoop tablespoon-sized portions of the chilled chocolate mixture and roll them into balls.
5. **Coat the truffles**: Roll each truffle in crushed peppermint candies, ensuring an even coating. Store in the refrigerator until ready to serve.

Apple Cider Donuts

Ingredients:

- 1 1/2 cups all-purpose flour
- 1 tsp baking powder
- 1/2 tsp baking soda
- 1/2 tsp ground cinnamon
- 1/4 tsp ground nutmeg
- 1/4 tsp salt
- 1/2 cup unsalted butter, softened
- 3/4 cup brown sugar
- 2 large eggs
- 1/2 cup apple cider
- 1 tsp vanilla extract
- Cinnamon sugar (for coating)

Instructions:

1. **Preheat the oven**: Set the oven to 350°F (175°C). Grease a donut pan.
2. **Mix dry ingredients**: In a bowl, whisk together the flour, baking powder, baking soda, cinnamon, nutmeg, and salt.
3. **Mix wet ingredients**: In another bowl, beat the butter and brown sugar until fluffy. Add the eggs, one at a time, mixing after each. Stir in the apple cider and vanilla extract.
4. **Combine and bake**: Gradually add the dry ingredients to the wet mixture and mix until smooth. Spoon the batter into the donut pan. Bake for 12-15 minutes or until a toothpick comes out clean.
5. **Coat the donuts**: Once cooled slightly, dip the donuts in cinnamon sugar.

Holiday Fruitcake

Ingredients:

- 2 cups mixed dried fruit (raisins, currants, chopped dried apricots, etc.)
- 1/2 cup chopped candied ginger
- 1/2 cup unsalted butter, softened
- 1 cup packed brown sugar
- 3 large eggs
- 1 1/2 cups all-purpose flour
- 1 tsp baking powder
- 1/2 tsp ground cinnamon
- 1/4 tsp ground nutmeg
- 1/2 cup chopped nuts (walnuts, pecans)
- 1/4 cup dark rum (optional)
- 1/4 cup orange juice

Instructions:

1. **Preheat the oven**: Set the oven to 325°F (165°C). Grease and line a loaf pan with parchment paper.
2. **Prepare the fruit**: In a small bowl, combine the dried fruit, candied ginger, and rum (if using). Let soak for 30 minutes.
3. **Mix wet ingredients**: In a large bowl, beat together the butter, sugar, and eggs until smooth. Add the orange juice.
4. **Combine dry ingredients**: In another bowl, whisk together the flour, baking powder, cinnamon, and nutmeg.
5. **Combine all ingredients**: Add the dry ingredients to the wet mixture, then fold in the soaked fruit and chopped nuts.
6. **Bake**: Pour the batter into the prepared pan and bake for 1 hour, or until a toothpick comes out clean. Let cool before serving.

Hot Cocoa Mix Jars

Ingredients:

- 1 1/2 cups powdered milk
- 1 cup unsweetened cocoa powder
- 1 cup powdered sugar
- 1/2 cup mini marshmallows
- 1/4 cup chocolate chips (optional)
- Mason jars for gift presentation

Instructions:

1. **Layer the ingredients**: In a mason jar, layer the powdered milk, cocoa powder, powdered sugar, and marshmallows. If desired, add a layer of chocolate chips.
2. **Seal and label**: Seal the jar and attach a label with instructions. For serving, mix 1/4 cup of the hot cocoa mix with 1 cup of hot water or milk.

Chocolate Toffee Bark

Ingredients:

- 1 cup unsalted butter
- 1 cup packed brown sugar
- 1/2 tsp vanilla extract
- 2 cups semisweet chocolate chips
- 1/2 cup chopped nuts (e.g., almonds, pecans)
- 1/4 tsp sea salt

Instructions:

1. **Prepare a baking sheet**:
   Line a baking sheet with parchment paper or a silicone baking mat.
2. **Make the toffee**:
   In a medium saucepan, melt the butter and brown sugar over medium heat, stirring constantly. Once the butter is melted, increase the heat and bring to a simmer. Cook for 3-4 minutes, allowing the mixture to thicken slightly.
3. **Pour the toffee**:
   Pour the toffee mixture over the prepared baking sheet, spreading it out evenly.
4. **Add chocolate**:
   Sprinkle the chocolate chips over the hot toffee. Let it sit for a few minutes to melt, then spread the chocolate into an even layer with a spatula.
5. **Add nuts and salt**:
   Sprinkle the chopped nuts and sea salt over the chocolate. Allow the bark to cool at room temperature, then refrigerate for 1 hour to set.
6. **Break into pieces**:
   Once fully set, break the bark into pieces and enjoy!

Cherry Almond Biscotti

Ingredients:

- 2 cups all-purpose flour
- 1 cup sugar
- 1 tsp baking powder
- 1/4 tsp salt
- 2 large eggs
- 1 tsp almond extract
- 1/2 cup dried cherries, chopped
- 1/2 cup sliced almonds

Instructions:

1. **Preheat oven and prepare baking sheet:**
   Preheat your oven to 350°F (175°C). Line a baking sheet with parchment paper.
2. **Mix dry ingredients:**
   In a large bowl, whisk together the flour, sugar, baking powder, and salt.
3. **Add wet ingredients:**
   In a separate bowl, whisk the eggs and almond extract. Pour the wet ingredients into the dry mixture and stir to form a dough.
4. **Incorporate cherries and almonds:**
   Fold in the chopped cherries and sliced almonds.
5. **Shape the dough:**
   Divide the dough in half and shape each half into a log, about 10 inches long, on the prepared baking sheet.
6. **Bake the logs:**
   Bake for 25-30 minutes, until golden brown. Remove from the oven and allow to cool for 10 minutes.
7. **Slice and bake again:**
   Slice each log into 1-inch wide pieces. Lay the slices flat on the baking sheet and bake for another 15-20 minutes until crisp.
8. **Cool and serve:**
   Allow the biscotti to cool completely before serving.

Pecan Pie Bars

Ingredients:

- **For the crust**:
    - 1 1/2 cups all-purpose flour
    - 1/2 cup unsalted butter, softened
    - 1/4 cup sugar
    - 1/4 tsp salt
- **For the filling**:
    - 1 cup light corn syrup
    - 1 cup packed brown sugar
    - 1/2 cup unsalted butter, melted
    - 3 large eggs
    - 1 tsp vanilla extract
    - 1/2 tsp salt
    - 2 cups pecans, chopped

Instructions:

1. **Preheat the oven**:
   Preheat the oven to 350°F (175°C). Grease a 9x13-inch baking pan or line it with parchment paper.
2. **Make the crust**:
   In a bowl, mix the flour, butter, sugar, and salt until the dough forms. Press the dough into the bottom of the prepared pan.
3. **Bake the crust**:
   Bake for 15-20 minutes, or until golden brown.
4. **Prepare the filling**:
   In a separate bowl, whisk together the corn syrup, brown sugar, melted butter, eggs, vanilla extract, and salt. Stir in the pecans.
5. **Fill the crust**:
   Pour the filling over the baked crust and spread it evenly.
6. **Bake the bars**:
   Bake for 25-30 minutes, or until the filling is set and lightly browned. Let cool completely before cutting into bars.

Eggnog Truffles

Ingredients:

- 8 oz white chocolate, chopped
- 1/2 cup eggnog
- 1 tbsp unsalted butter
- 1/4 tsp ground nutmeg
- 1/2 tsp vanilla extract
- 1/2 cup finely chopped white chocolate (for coating)

Instructions:

1. **Melt the chocolate**:
   In a heatproof bowl, melt the white chocolate and eggnog together over a double boiler or in the microwave, stirring every 30 seconds.
2. **Add flavorings**:
   Stir in the butter, nutmeg, and vanilla extract. Mix until smooth.
3. **Chill the mixture**:
   Refrigerate the mixture for about 2 hours, or until firm enough to scoop.
4. **Form truffles**:
   Use a spoon to scoop out small portions of the chilled mixture and roll them into balls.
5. **Coat the truffles**:
   Roll each truffle in the finely chopped white chocolate.
6. **Chill and serve**:
   Return the truffles to the refrigerator to set before serving.

Molasses Cookies

Ingredients:

- 2 1/4 cups all-purpose flour
- 1 tsp baking soda
- 1/2 tsp ground ginger
- 1/2 tsp ground cinnamon
- 1/4 tsp ground cloves
- 1/4 tsp salt
- 3/4 cup unsalted butter, softened
- 1 cup sugar, plus extra for rolling
- 1 large egg
- 1/4 cup molasses

Instructions:

1. **Preheat the oven**:
   Preheat the oven to 350°F (175°C). Line a baking sheet with parchment paper.
2. **Mix dry ingredients**:
   In a bowl, whisk together the flour, baking soda, ginger, cinnamon, cloves, and salt.
3. **Cream the butter and sugar**:
   In a separate bowl, beat the butter and sugar together until fluffy. Add the egg and molasses and mix until combined.
4. **Add dry ingredients**:
   Gradually add the dry ingredients to the wet mixture and stir until just combined.
5. **Shape the cookies**:
   Roll the dough into 1-inch balls and roll each ball in sugar.
6. **Bake the cookies**:
   Place the balls on the baking sheet and bake for 8-10 minutes, or until they are slightly cracked on top. Allow them to cool on a wire rack.

Salted Caramel Brownies

Ingredients:

- **For the brownies:**
    - 1/2 cup unsalted butter, melted
    - 1 cup sugar
    - 2 large eggs
    - 1 tsp vanilla extract
    - 1/3 cup cocoa powder
    - 1/2 cup all-purpose flour
    - 1/4 tsp salt
- **For the salted caramel:**
    - 1/2 cup heavy cream
    - 1/2 cup sugar
    - 1/4 cup unsalted butter
    - 1/4 tsp sea salt

Instructions:

1. **Preheat the oven:**
   Preheat the oven to 350°F (175°C). Grease a 9x9-inch baking pan.
2. **Make the brownie batter:**
   In a large bowl, mix together the melted butter, sugar, eggs, and vanilla extract. Stir in the cocoa powder, flour, and salt.
3. **Bake the brownies:**
   Pour the brownie batter into the prepared pan and bake for 20-25 minutes, or until a toothpick comes out clean.
4. **Make the caramel:**
   In a saucepan, combine the cream, sugar, butter, and sea salt. Cook over medium heat until the mixture comes to a boil. Simmer for 5 minutes, stirring constantly.
5. **Assemble:**
   Once the brownies are baked, pour the caramel over the top and let it cool before cutting into squares.

Candy Cane Macarons

Ingredients:

- 1 cup powdered sugar
- 1 cup almond flour
- 3 large egg whites
- 1/4 cup granulated sugar
- 1/2 tsp peppermint extract
- 1/4 cup crushed candy canes
- **For the filling**:
    - 1/2 cup butter, softened
    - 1 cup powdered sugar
    - 1/4 tsp peppermint extract

Instructions:

1. **Prepare the macarons**:
   Preheat the oven to 300°F (150°C). Line a baking sheet with parchment paper. In a food processor, pulse the powdered sugar and almond flour until finely ground.
2. **Whip the egg whites**:
   In a clean bowl, whisk the egg whites until soft peaks form. Gradually add the granulated sugar and whisk until stiff peaks form. Fold in the peppermint extract.
3. **Fold in the dry ingredients**:
   Gently fold in the almond flour mixture until just combined.
4. **Pipe the macarons**:
   Pipe the batter onto the prepared baking sheet in small, even circles. Tap the baking sheet on the counter to release air bubbles. Sprinkle crushed candy canes on top.
5. **Bake**:
   Bake the macarons for 15-18 minutes. Let them cool completely.
6. **Make the filling**:
   Beat together the butter, powdered sugar, and peppermint extract. Sandwich the filling between two macarons.

Hazelnut Chocolate Tartlets

Ingredients:

- 1 1/2 cups crushed graham crackers or cookies
- 1/4 cup melted butter
- 1/2 cup hazelnut spread (Nutella)
- 3/4 cup heavy cream
- 1/2 cup dark chocolate chips
- 1/2 cup chopped hazelnuts

Instructions:

1. **Prepare the crust**:
   Mix the crushed graham crackers and melted butter. Press the mixture into tartlet pans.
2. **Make the filling**:
   Heat the cream in a saucepan until it begins to simmer. Pour the cream over the chocolate chips and stir until smooth. Add the hazelnut spread and mix well.
3. **Assemble the tartlets**:
   Spoon the chocolate hazelnut mixture into the crusts. Top with chopped hazelnuts.
4. **Chill**:
   Refrigerate the tartlets for at least 2 hours to set before serving.

Gingerbread Fudge

Ingredients:

- 2 cups white chocolate chips
- 1/2 cup sweetened condensed milk
- 1/4 cup molasses
- 1/2 tsp ground ginger
- 1/2 tsp ground cinnamon
- 1/4 tsp ground cloves
- 1/4 tsp ground nutmeg
- 1/4 tsp salt

Instructions:

1. **Prepare the pan**:
   Line an 8x8-inch baking pan with parchment paper.
2. **Melt the fudge base**:
   In a medium saucepan, combine the white chocolate chips, sweetened condensed milk, and molasses. Heat over low to medium heat, stirring constantly until smooth and melted.
3. **Add spices**:
   Stir in the ginger, cinnamon, cloves, nutmeg, and salt. Continue to mix until everything is evenly incorporated.
4. **Pour and chill**:
   Pour the fudge mixture into the prepared baking pan and spread it into an even layer. Refrigerate for at least 2 hours, or until fully set.
5. **Cut and serve**:
   Once the fudge has set, remove from the pan and cut into squares to serve.

Caramel Pecan Pretzel Bites

Ingredients:

- 1 bag small pretzels
- 1 cup caramel bits (or caramel candies)
- 1/2 cup heavy cream
- 1 cup pecans, roughly chopped
- Sea salt, for sprinkling

Instructions:

1. **Prepare the pretzels**:
   Preheat the oven to 350°F (175°C). Place the pretzels in a single layer on a baking sheet.
2. **Make the caramel**:
   In a small saucepan, heat the caramel bits and heavy cream over medium heat. Stir occasionally until the caramel is completely melted and smooth.
3. **Assemble the bites**:
   Spoon a small amount of caramel over each pretzel, then top with chopped pecans.
4. **Bake**:
   Bake for about 5 minutes, or until the caramel is bubbly and the pretzels are warm.
5. **Cool and sprinkle**:
   Remove from the oven and sprinkle with a pinch of sea salt. Let the bites cool before serving.

Mini Cheesecakes with Cranberry Sauce

Ingredients:

- **For the cheesecake:**
    - 8 oz cream cheese, softened
    - 1/2 cup sugar
    - 1 tsp vanilla extract
    - 1 large egg
    - 1/2 cup sour cream
- **For the crust:**
    - 1 cup graham cracker crumbs
    - 1/4 cup melted butter
    - 1/4 cup sugar
- **For the cranberry sauce:**
    - 1 cup fresh cranberries
    - 1/4 cup sugar
    - 1/4 cup water

Instructions:

1. **Prepare the crust:**
   Preheat the oven to 325°F (160°C). In a bowl, combine the graham cracker crumbs, melted butter, and sugar. Press the mixture into the bottoms of mini cheesecake pans or muffin tins lined with paper liners.
2. **Make the cheesecake filling:**
   In a separate bowl, beat together the cream cheese, sugar, vanilla extract, and egg until smooth. Add the sour cream and mix until combined.
3. **Assemble the cheesecakes:**
   Pour the cheesecake mixture over the crusts in the mini pans. Bake for 20-25 minutes, or until the cheesecakes are set and the tops are slightly golden. Let them cool to room temperature, then refrigerate for at least 2 hours.
4. **Make the cranberry sauce:**
   In a saucepan, combine the cranberries, sugar, and water. Cook over medium heat until the cranberries burst and the sauce thickens, about 10 minutes. Let it cool.
5. **Serve:**
   Top each mini cheesecake with a spoonful of cranberry sauce before serving.

Poppy Seed Lemon Muffins

Ingredients:

- 1 1/2 cups all-purpose flour
- 1 cup sugar
- 1/2 tsp baking powder
- 1/2 tsp baking soda
- 1/4 tsp salt
- 2 tbsp poppy seeds
- 1/2 cup sour cream
- 1/4 cup vegetable oil
- 2 large eggs
- 1/4 cup fresh lemon juice
- 1 tsp lemon zest
- 1/2 tsp vanilla extract

Instructions:

1. **Preheat the oven:**
   Preheat your oven to 350°F (175°C). Line a muffin tin with paper liners.
2. **Mix dry ingredients:**
   In a bowl, whisk together the flour, sugar, baking powder, baking soda, salt, and poppy seeds.
3. **Mix wet ingredients:**
   In another bowl, whisk together the sour cream, vegetable oil, eggs, lemon juice, lemon zest, and vanilla extract.
4. **Combine and bake:**
   Fold the wet ingredients into the dry ingredients until just combined. Spoon the batter into the muffin tin, filling each cup about 2/3 full.
5. **Bake:**
   Bake for 18-20 minutes, or until a toothpick inserted into the center comes out clean. Let the muffins cool on a wire rack.

Spiced Hot Chocolate Cookies

Ingredients:

- 1 1/2 cups all-purpose flour
- 1/2 cup cocoa powder
- 1 tsp baking powder
- 1/4 tsp salt
- 1/2 tsp ground cinnamon
- 1/4 tsp ground nutmeg
- 1/4 tsp ground ginger
- 1 cup unsalted butter, softened
- 1 cup brown sugar
- 1 large egg
- 1 tsp vanilla extract
- 1/4 cup hot cocoa mix
- 1/2 cup mini marshmallows (optional)

Instructions:

1. **Preheat the oven**:
   Preheat the oven to 350°F (175°C). Line a baking sheet with parchment paper.
2. **Mix dry ingredients**:
   In a bowl, whisk together the flour, cocoa powder, baking powder, salt, cinnamon, nutmeg, ginger, and hot cocoa mix.
3. **Make the dough**:
   In another bowl, beat the butter and brown sugar until light and fluffy. Add the egg and vanilla extract and mix well. Gradually add the dry ingredients and stir until combined.
4. **Shape the cookies**:
   Drop spoonfuls of dough onto the prepared baking sheet. If desired, gently press a few mini marshmallows into the top of each cookie.
5. **Bake**:
   Bake for 10-12 minutes, or until the edges are set. Allow the cookies to cool on the baking sheet for a few minutes before transferring them to a wire rack.

Chai Spiced Cupcakes

Ingredients:

- 1 1/2 cups all-purpose flour
- 1 tsp baking powder
- 1/2 tsp ground cinnamon
- 1/2 tsp ground ginger
- 1/4 tsp ground cardamom
- 1/4 tsp ground cloves
- 1/4 tsp ground black pepper
- 1/2 cup unsalted butter, softened
- 1 cup sugar
- 2 large eggs
- 1 tsp vanilla extract
- 1/2 cup milk

Instructions:

1. **Preheat the oven**:
   Preheat the oven to 350°F (175°C). Line a muffin tin with paper liners.
2. **Mix dry ingredients**:
   In a bowl, whisk together the flour, baking powder, cinnamon, ginger, cardamom, cloves, and black pepper.
3. **Make the batter**:
   In another bowl, beat the butter and sugar until creamy. Add the eggs one at a time, mixing well after each. Stir in the vanilla extract. Gradually add the dry ingredients, alternating with the milk, and mix until smooth.
4. **Bake**:
   Spoon the batter into the muffin tin, filling each cup about 2/3 full. Bake for 18-20 minutes, or until a toothpick inserted into the center comes out clean. Let the cupcakes cool.

Cinnamon Sugar Roasted Nuts

Ingredients:

- 2 cups mixed nuts (e.g., almonds, cashews, walnuts)
- 1/4 cup maple syrup
- 1 tbsp cinnamon
- 1/4 tsp ground ginger
- 1/4 tsp ground nutmeg
- 1/4 tsp salt

Instructions:

1. **Preheat the oven**:
   Preheat the oven to 350°F (175°C). Line a baking sheet with parchment paper.
2. **Coat the nuts**:
   In a large bowl, toss the nuts with maple syrup, cinnamon, ginger, nutmeg, and salt until evenly coated.
3. **Roast the nuts**:
   Spread the nuts in a single layer on the baking sheet. Roast for 15-20 minutes, stirring once halfway through, until the nuts are golden and fragrant.
4. **Cool and serve**:
   Let the roasted nuts cool completely before serving.

Maple Glazed Donuts

Ingredients:

- 2 cups all-purpose flour
- 1 tsp baking powder
- 1/2 tsp baking soda
- 1/4 tsp salt
- 1/2 tsp ground cinnamon
- 1/2 cup buttermilk
- 1/4 cup maple syrup
- 2 large eggs
- 1/4 cup unsalted butter, melted
- **For the glaze**:
    - 1/2 cup powdered sugar
    - 2 tbsp maple syrup
    - 1 tbsp milk

Instructions:

1. **Preheat the oven**:
   Preheat the oven to 350°F (175°C). Grease a donut pan.
2. **Mix dry ingredients**:
   In a bowl, whisk together the flour, baking powder, baking soda, salt, and cinnamon.
3. **Mix wet ingredients**:
   In another bowl, whisk together the buttermilk, maple syrup, eggs, and melted butter.
4. **Combine and bake**:
   Add the wet ingredients to the dry ingredients and mix until smooth. Spoon the batter into the donut pan. Bake for 12-15 minutes, or until a toothpick inserted comes out clean.
5. **Make the glaze**:
   In a small bowl, whisk together the powdered sugar, maple syrup, and milk.
6. **Glaze and serve**:
   Dip each donut into the glaze and place it on a wire rack to set.

Almond Joy Fudge

Ingredients:

- 2 cups white chocolate chips
- 1/2 cup sweetened condensed milk
- 1/4 cup coconut flakes
- 1/2 cup whole almonds
- 1/2 cup semi-sweet chocolate chips

Instructions:

1. **Prepare the pan**:
   Line an 8x8-inch baking pan with parchment paper.
2. **Melt the white chocolate**:
   In a saucepan over low heat, melt the white chocolate chips and sweetened condensed milk together. Stir constantly until smooth and creamy.
3. **Add coconut**:
   Once the mixture is smooth, fold in the coconut flakes and stir until evenly combined.
4. **Assemble the fudge**:
   Pour the mixture into the prepared pan and spread it evenly. Place the almonds on top, pressing them gently into the fudge.
5. **Top with chocolate**:
   Melt the semi-sweet chocolate chips and drizzle them over the fudge. Use a toothpick to swirl the chocolate into the fudge for a marbled effect.
6. **Chill**:
   Refrigerate the fudge for 2-3 hours, or until set. Once firm, cut into squares and serve.

Roasted Chestnuts

Ingredients:

- 1 lb chestnuts
- 1 tbsp olive oil
- Salt to taste

Instructions:

1. **Preheat the oven:**
   Preheat your oven to 400°F (200°C).
2. **Score the chestnuts:**
   Using a sharp knife, score an "X" on the flat side of each chestnut.
3. **Roast the chestnuts:**
   Place the chestnuts on a baking sheet and drizzle with olive oil. Roast for 20-25 minutes, or until the shells peel back and the nuts are tender.
4. **Peel and serve:**
   Once the chestnuts are cool enough to handle, peel off the shells and serve with a sprinkle of salt.

Holiday Cake Pops

Ingredients:

- 1 box cake mix (or homemade cake)
- 1/2 cup frosting (store-bought or homemade)
- Candy melts or chocolate for coating
- Sprinkles or decorations for garnish

Instructions:

1. **Bake the cake:**
   Bake the cake according to the package instructions or your homemade recipe. Let it cool completely.
2. **Crumble the cake:**
   Once the cake is cool, crumble it into small pieces in a large bowl.
3. **Mix with frosting:**
   Add frosting to the cake crumbs and mix until the mixture holds together when pressed.
4. **Shape the cake pops:**
   Roll the cake mixture into small balls (about 1 inch in diameter). Insert a cake pop stick into each ball.
5. **Coat with candy melts:**
   Melt the candy melts or chocolate and dip each cake pop into the melted coating. Sprinkle with festive decorations or sprinkles.
6. **Cool and serve:**
   Place the cake pops on a stand or a block of foam to cool completely.

Cranberry Pistachio Shortbread

Ingredients:

- 2 cups all-purpose flour
- 1/2 cup powdered sugar
- 1 cup unsalted butter, softened
- 1/2 tsp vanilla extract
- 1/2 cup dried cranberries, chopped
- 1/2 cup pistachios, chopped

Instructions:

1. **Preheat the oven:**
   Preheat your oven to 350°F (175°C). Line a baking sheet with parchment paper.
2. **Make the dough:**
   In a large bowl, beat together the butter, powdered sugar, and vanilla extract until smooth. Gradually add the flour and mix until a dough forms.
3. **Add cranberries and pistachios:**
   Fold in the chopped cranberries and pistachios.
4. **Shape the cookies:**
   Roll the dough into 1-inch balls and place them on the prepared baking sheet. Press each cookie gently with a fork or your fingers.
5. **Bake:**
   Bake for 10-12 minutes, or until the edges are lightly golden. Let cool on a wire rack.

Chocolate Peppermint Whoopie Pies

Ingredients:

- **For the cookies**:
    - 1 1/2 cups all-purpose flour
    - 1/2 cup unsweetened cocoa powder
    - 1 tsp baking soda
    - 1/4 tsp salt
    - 1/2 cup unsalted butter, softened
    - 1 cup sugar
    - 1 large egg
    - 1 tsp vanilla extract
    - 1/2 cup buttermilk
    - 1/2 tsp peppermint extract
- **For the filling**:
    - 1/2 cup unsalted butter, softened
    - 1 1/2 cups powdered sugar
    - 1/2 tsp peppermint extract
    - 2 tbsp milk

Instructions:

1. **Preheat the oven**:
   Preheat the oven to 350°F (175°C). Line a baking sheet with parchment paper.
2. **Make the cookies**:
   In a bowl, whisk together the flour, cocoa powder, baking soda, and salt. In another bowl, beat the butter and sugar until creamy. Add the egg and vanilla extract, mixing until smooth. Gradually add the dry ingredients, alternating with the buttermilk, and mix until combined. Stir in the peppermint extract.
3. **Bake the cookies**:
   Drop spoonfuls of dough onto the baking sheet, spacing them about 2 inches apart. Bake for 8-10 minutes, or until a toothpick comes out clean. Let the cookies cool completely.
4. **Make the filling**:
   Beat together the butter, powdered sugar, peppermint extract, and milk until smooth and fluffy.
5. **Assemble the whoopie pies**:
   Spread a generous amount of filling on the flat side of one cookie and top with another cookie to form a sandwich. Repeat with the remaining cookies.

Pumpkin Spice Truffles

Ingredients:

- 1/2 cup canned pumpkin puree
- 1 1/2 cups white chocolate chips
- 1/2 tsp ground cinnamon
- 1/4 tsp ground nutmeg
- 1/4 tsp ground ginger
- 1/2 cup crushed graham crackers (for coating)

Instructions:

1. **Melt the chocolate:**
   In a heatproof bowl, melt the white chocolate chips over a double boiler or in the microwave, stirring until smooth.
2. **Mix the pumpkin and spices:**
   Stir the pumpkin puree, cinnamon, nutmeg, and ginger into the melted chocolate.
3. **Chill the mixture:**
   Allow the mixture to cool to room temperature, then refrigerate for about 1 hour until firm enough to roll into balls.
4. **Form the truffles:**
   Roll the mixture into small balls, then roll them in crushed graham crackers.
5. **Chill and serve:**
   Refrigerate the truffles until set, about 30 minutes, before serving.

Butterscotch Pretzel Cookies

Ingredients:

- 1 1/2 cups all-purpose flour
- 1/2 tsp baking soda
- 1/4 tsp salt
- 1/2 cup unsalted butter, softened
- 1 cup brown sugar
- 1 large egg
- 1 tsp vanilla extract
- 1/2 cup butterscotch chips
- 1/2 cup crushed pretzels

Instructions:

1. **Preheat the oven**:
   Preheat the oven to 350°F (175°C). Line a baking sheet with parchment paper.
2. **Make the dough**:
   In a bowl, whisk together the flour, baking soda, and salt. In another bowl, beat the butter and brown sugar until light and fluffy. Add the egg and vanilla extract and mix well. Gradually add the dry ingredients and mix until combined.
3. **Add the chips and pretzels**:
   Fold in the butterscotch chips and crushed pretzels.
4. **Bake**:
   Drop spoonfuls of dough onto the baking sheet and bake for 10-12 minutes, or until golden brown. Let cool on a wire rack.

Sweet Potato Pie Bars

Ingredients:

- **For the crust:**
    - 1 1/2 cups graham cracker crumbs
    - 1/4 cup melted butter
    - 1/4 cup sugar
- **For the filling:**
    - 2 cups mashed sweet potatoes
    - 1 cup brown sugar
    - 1 tsp vanilla extract
    - 1 tsp ground cinnamon
    - 1/2 tsp ground nutmeg
    - 1/2 tsp ground ginger
    - 3 large eggs
    - 1/2 cup evaporated milk

Instructions:

1. **Make the crust:**
   Preheat the oven to 350°F (175°C). Combine the graham cracker crumbs, melted butter, and sugar. Press the mixture into the bottom of a greased 9x13-inch baking dish.
2. **Make the filling:**
   In a bowl, combine the mashed sweet potatoes, brown sugar, vanilla, cinnamon, nutmeg, and ginger. Beat in the eggs and evaporated milk until smooth.
3. **Assemble and bake:**
   Pour the filling over the crust and bake for 40-45 minutes, or until the filling is set and a toothpick comes out clean. Let cool before cutting into bars.

Mocha Mint Brownies

Ingredients:

- **For the brownies**:
    - 1 cup unsalted butter
    - 1 cup sugar
    - 1 cup cocoa powder
    - 4 large eggs
    - 1 tsp vanilla extract
    - 1/2 tsp peppermint extract
    - 1/2 cup all-purpose flour
    - 1/4 tsp salt
    - 1/4 tsp baking powder
    - 1/2 cup brewed coffee (cooled)
- **For the topping**:
    - 1 cup powdered sugar
    - 2 tbsp unsalted butter
    - 1/2 tsp peppermint extract
    - 1-2 tbsp milk
    - Crushed chocolate mints (optional)

Instructions:

1. **Make the brownies**:
   Preheat the oven to 350°F (175°C). Grease and line a 9x9-inch baking pan. Melt the butter in a bowl, then stir in the sugar and cocoa powder. Add the eggs, vanilla, and peppermint extract. Mix in the flour, salt, and baking powder, then stir in the coffee.
2. **Bake**:
   Pour the brownie batter into the prepared pan and bake for 30-35 minutes, or until a toothpick comes out clean.
3. **Make the topping**:
   In a bowl, mix the powdered sugar, butter, peppermint extract, and milk until smooth. Spread the topping over the cooled brownies and sprinkle with crushed chocolate mints if desired.

Eggnog Panna Cotta

Ingredients:

- 2 cups eggnog
- 1 cup heavy cream
- 1/4 cup sugar
- 1 packet unflavored gelatin
- 1 tsp vanilla extract
- 1/4 tsp ground nutmeg
- 1/4 tsp ground cinnamon

Instructions:

1. **Prepare the gelatin:**
   In a small bowl, sprinkle the gelatin over 2 tablespoons of cold water. Let it bloom for about 5 minutes.
2. **Heat the eggnog and cream:**
   In a saucepan, combine the eggnog, heavy cream, and sugar. Heat over medium heat until the sugar dissolves and the mixture is warm, but not boiling.
3. **Add the gelatin:**
   Once the eggnog mixture is warm, remove from heat and stir in the bloomed gelatin until it dissolves completely.
4. **Flavor the panna cotta:**
   Stir in the vanilla extract, nutmeg, and cinnamon.
5. **Set the panna cotta:**
   Pour the mixture into serving glasses or molds. Refrigerate for at least 4 hours or until set.
6. **Serve:**
   Serve with a sprinkle of nutmeg or cinnamon on top.

Cranberry Meringue Cookies

Ingredients:

- 3 large egg whites
- 1/4 tsp cream of tartar
- 3/4 cup sugar
- 1/2 tsp vanilla extract
- 1/2 cup dried cranberries, chopped

Instructions:

1. **Preheat the oven**:
   Preheat the oven to 250°F (120°C). Line a baking sheet with parchment paper.
2. **Whisk the egg whites**:
   In a large bowl, whisk the egg whites with the cream of tartar until soft peaks form.
3. **Add sugar**:
   Gradually add the sugar, 1 tablespoon at a time, and continue whisking until stiff peaks form and the mixture is glossy.
4. **Fold in vanilla and cranberries**:
   Gently fold in the vanilla extract and chopped cranberries.
5. **Pipe the meringues**:
   Spoon or pipe the meringue mixture onto the prepared baking sheet in small dollops.
6. **Bake**:
   Bake for 1 hour, or until the meringues are crisp and can easily be lifted off the parchment paper. Let cool completely.

Chocolate-Covered Caramel Apples

Ingredients:

- 6 small apples
- 1 bag caramel candies
- 1 tbsp milk
- 1 1/2 cups semisweet chocolate chips
- 1/4 cup chopped nuts or sprinkles (optional)

Instructions:

1. **Prepare the apples**:
   Wash and dry the apples. Insert a wooden stick into each apple.
2. **Melt the caramel**:
   Unwrap the caramel candies and melt them with the milk in a heatproof bowl over low heat or in the microwave, stirring occasionally until smooth.
3. **Dip in caramel**:
   Dip each apple into the melted caramel, turning to coat. Let the excess drip off and place the apples on a parchment-lined baking sheet.
4. **Melt the chocolate**:
   Melt the chocolate chips in a heatproof bowl over low heat or in the microwave, stirring until smooth.
5. **Dip in chocolate**:
   Once the caramel has set, dip the apples into the melted chocolate, allowing any excess to drip off. Add chopped nuts or sprinkles if desired.
6. **Cool and serve**:
   Let the apples cool on the baking sheet until the chocolate hardens.

Spiced Apple Cider Caramels

Ingredients:

- 1 cup apple cider
- 1/2 cup heavy cream
- 1 cup unsalted butter
- 2 cups brown sugar
- 1/2 cup corn syrup
- 1/2 tsp ground cinnamon
- 1/4 tsp ground cloves
- 1/4 tsp ground nutmeg
- 1/2 tsp vanilla extract

Instructions:

1. **Cook the apple cider:**
   In a saucepan, bring the apple cider to a boil over medium-high heat. Reduce the heat and simmer until the cider is reduced by half.
2. **Make the caramel:**
   Add the heavy cream, butter, brown sugar, corn syrup, cinnamon, cloves, and nutmeg to the saucepan. Stir to combine and bring to a boil. Cook, stirring frequently, until the mixture reaches 245°F (118°C) on a candy thermometer.
3. **Cool the caramel:**
   Remove the saucepan from heat and stir in the vanilla extract. Pour the caramel into a greased 9x9-inch baking pan.
4. **Set the caramels:**
   Let the caramel cool completely before cutting it into small squares.

Mint Chocolate Chip Cookies

Ingredients:

- 1 1/2 cups all-purpose flour
- 1/2 tsp baking soda
- 1/4 tsp salt
- 1/2 cup unsalted butter, softened
- 1/2 cup sugar
- 1/2 cup brown sugar
- 1 large egg
- 1 tsp peppermint extract
- 1 cup semi-sweet chocolate chips
- 1/2 cup mini chocolate chips
- 1/2 cup crushed peppermint candies

Instructions:

1. **Preheat the oven**:
   Preheat the oven to 350°F (175°C). Line a baking sheet with parchment paper.
2. **Mix the dry ingredients**:
   In a small bowl, whisk together the flour, baking soda, and salt.
3. **Cream the butter and sugars**:
   In a large bowl, beat the butter, sugar, and brown sugar until light and fluffy. Add the egg and peppermint extract and mix well.
4. **Combine the ingredients**:
   Gradually add the dry ingredients to the wet ingredients and stir until combined. Fold in the chocolate chips, mini chocolate chips, and crushed peppermint candies.
5. **Shape and bake**:
   Drop spoonfuls of dough onto the prepared baking sheet. Bake for 10-12 minutes or until golden brown. Let cool on a wire rack.

Cranberry Coconut Macaroons

Ingredients:

- 2 large egg whites
- 1/4 tsp cream of tartar
- 1/2 cup sugar
- 1 1/2 cups shredded coconut
- 1/2 cup dried cranberries, chopped

Instructions:

1. **Preheat the oven:**
   Preheat the oven to 325°F (160°C). Line a baking sheet with parchment paper.
2. **Whisk the egg whites:**
   In a bowl, whisk the egg whites and cream of tartar until soft peaks form. Gradually add the sugar, continuing to whisk until stiff peaks form.
3. **Fold in coconut and cranberries:**
   Gently fold in the shredded coconut and chopped cranberries.
4. **Shape the macaroons:**
   Spoon the mixture onto the prepared baking sheet, forming small mounds.
5. **Bake:**
   Bake for 15-20 minutes, or until the edges are golden brown. Let cool completely.

Chocolate Dipped Fruit

Ingredients:

- 1 cup semisweet or milk chocolate chips
- 2 cups mixed fresh fruit (strawberries, orange slices, apple slices, etc.)

Instructions:

1. **Melt the chocolate**:
   Melt the chocolate chips in a heatproof bowl over low heat or in the microwave, stirring occasionally until smooth.
2. **Dip the fruit**:
   Dip each piece of fruit into the melted chocolate, coating it halfway or entirely as desired.
3. **Set the fruit**:
   Place the dipped fruit on a parchment-lined tray and let the chocolate harden. Refrigerate if needed to speed up the process.

Festive Marzipan Treats

Ingredients:

- 2 cups almond flour
- 1 cup powdered sugar
- 1 egg white
- 1 tsp almond extract
- Food coloring (optional)

Instructions:

1. **Make the marzipan**:
   In a food processor, combine the almond flour, powdered sugar, egg white, and almond extract. Process until the mixture forms a smooth dough.
2. **Shape the marzipan**:
   Divide the dough into small portions and add food coloring if desired. Shape the dough into small balls, logs, or festive shapes using cookie cutters.
3. **Decorate and serve**:
   Decorate the marzipan treats with edible glitter or sugar if desired. Serve or store in an airtight container.

www.ingramcontent.com/pod-product-compliance
Lightning Source LLC
LaVergne TN
LVHW081339060526
838201LV00055B/2738